D0397219

post scripts
humor

the curtis publishing company,
indianapolis, indiana

post scripts humor

cartoons, puns, poems, and pithy prose from *THE SATURDAY EVENING POST*

Post Scripts Humor
Editors: Jean White and Michael Morris
Designer: Jinny B. Sauer
Art and production staff: Marianne Roan,
Kay Douglas, Steve Miller and Dwight Lamb
Editorial staff: Louise Fortson and John D. Craton
Compositors: Marie Caldwell, Gloria McCoy, Geri Watson
and Penny Allison

 Printed in The United States of America. For information address The Curtis Publishing Company, Inc., 1100 Waterway Boulevard, Indianapolis, Indiana 46202. Library of Congress Catalog Card Number 78-53039
ISBN 0-89387-022-6.

table of contents

all in the family

Sage Advice

"Grandmother, what kind of husband would you advise me to get?"

"My advice is to leave the husbands alone, and get yourself a single man."

—*Lucille Harper*

Trampled Moral

As my son and I watched some ants busily crawling over the ground, collecting and carrying smidgeons of food to their hill, I decided it was a good time to deliver a lecture on industry. "Ants work harder than almost any creature alive," I orated. "All summer long, they keep busy storing up food for winter." Then, thinking I'd made my point, I asked, "And what do you suppose ants get for all the work they do?"

Cynically, the boy answered, "Stepped on."

—*Margaret Shauers*

"Oh, there you are, dear . . . we were just talking about you."

The Father and Son Talk

He asked his father
Where the birds had come from,
And Father thought, "Ah,
Yes, the right time has come."
He began to explain
The story of life.
(They'd been expecting this—
Both he and his wife.)
The father talked on.
The boy soon looked bored.
Still, Dad continued
(Now largely ignored).
At last, a pause, then
With tolerant affection,
The boy said, "But, Dad,
I meant *which direction?*"

—*Anne McCarroll*

Silence Is Golden

This couple had a little boy who refused to talk. He wouldn't even try.

Worried, his parents took him to all kinds of doctors

who could find no reason for the child's failure to speak.

Then, one evening when he was about six years old, the boy pushed away his dinner plate and said plainly, "This food is lousy!"

His parents were jubilant. "Junior! You can speak. You can speak! Tell us, how does it happen you have never said anything before?"

Junior shrugged his shoulders. "Well," he said, "up to now everything's been okay."

—Beth Cook

"Oh, pretty good, Frank, how's it been with you?"

She Saw Him Do It.

Small boy's definition of a conscience: Something that makes you tell your mother before your sister does.

—Lucille S. Harper

Angelic Flight

Grandparents have advantages
That younger parents lack.
They seldom scold the tiny tots;
They never scream or smack . . .
When little angels misbehave,
They send the darlings back.

—Nova Trimble Ashley

To My Help-Spend

You're perfect, dear, in every way—
Congenial and consortable;
But when I get your bills to pay,
I find you insupportable.

—Norman R. Jaffray

"Mom, don't change the baby. I like her just the way she is."

From Genes to Jeans

As I study both my offspring
In patched-up, faded jeans,
And cope with their rebellion
In angry, tearful scene,
I wish that I could analyze
The *chemistry* of teens—
Which hang-ups can we blame on *peers*,
And which ones came from *genes*?

—*Corinne Adria Bariteau*

"I don't remember when I've seen a better presentation."

Vacation Destination

Some like it cold, some like it hot.
One likes the ocean, one does not.
Throughout history, it hasn't varied.
Inevitably the two are married.

—Gail Cooke

Cooperative Baby

The nickel-nursing Smiths took their infant son to a movie. The usher warned them that unless the baby remained quiet, the management would refund their money and ask them to leave.

Near the end of the feature, Smith nudged his wife and whispered, "What do you think of it?"

"Terrible," replied Mrs. Smith.

"Check," agreed Smith. "Pinch the baby."

—H. L. Pritchard

Conversations

"I'm sure you'll like Jack," the daughter said to her father. "He's a very nice young man."

"Has he got any money?" her father asked.

"Oh, you men are all alike," she said indignantly. "He asked the same thing about you."

—*Lucille S. Harper*

Ain't That A Shame

There was a young man from Peoria
Who said to a girl: "I adoreia,
Your form and your face
Have such beauty and grace—
But my wife just won't let me see moreia."

—*A. S. Flaumenhaft*

"Never mind how we get our sheets so white, is this or isn't this your husband?"

Tough Question

Having a "father-and-son" talk with his youngster, the father stated, "The trouble with you, son, is that you are always wishing for things you haven't got."

"But, Dad . . . what else are you supposed to wish for?" questioned the youngster.

—Lucille J. Goodyear

Lines for an Ex-Husband

He was a devoted health food fan,
A blackstrap molasses and wheat germ man.
He poured her coffee down the sink
And gave her a vinegar-honey drink.
(She didn't want to be a critic,
But it never cured her pain arthritic.)
Hors d'oeuvres for their Thanksgiving feast
He sprinkled with kelp and brewer's yeast;
And they went on a New Year's bender
With parsley and eggshells juiced by blender.
He was a faithful Valentine giver—
Of candy-coated desiccated liver!
Ah, but she could have endured all this;
They might still be sharing healthful bliss.
She never might have blown the scene
And sought the single life afar
Had she not discovered in his car
That plastic spoon from Dairy Queen!

—Marcella Siegel

All in the Family

Prospective father-in-law: "Young man, can you support a family?"

Prospective groom: "Well, no, sir, I was just planning to support your daughter. The rest of you will have to shift for yourselves."

—Rose Sands

"Now remember, I'm only five years old."

Litterly Speaking

A splash of grease, a drop of jam,
A stick of candy, crush of graham.
I don't excel in household chores,
But guests can eat right off my floors.

—Ellie Womack

Preparing for the Future

Every young man should learn to take criticism. He'll probably be a parent someday.

—Franklin P. Jones

"This really works out great, dear! I just couldn't think of what to give you for your birthday!"

Puzzling

Some couples live together with never a cross word. Then there are couples who are still on speaking terms.

—*Hal Chadwick*

Master or Slave?

The little boy was given a full-grown St. Bernard for his birthday. Looking at his prize with delight and wonder, he asked his Daddy, "Is he mine, or am I his?"

—*Samuel J. Stannard*

Distressing Dressing

The young married couple were having their first turkey dinner at home. "Just think, honey," the wife said proudly, "I prepared this turkey all by myself."

"And what about the stuffing—did you make it yourself?"

"Oh, I didn't have to," replied the bride. "This one wasn't hollow."

—Dorothea Kent

My True Love Gave to Me

After 30 days of summer camp
My kid returned to me:
Nine shredded T-shirts,
Eight garter snakes,
Seven pounds of rocks,
Six filthy towels,
Five torn swimsuits,
Four wet pajamas,
Three live toads,
Two cans of worms
And a rash from a poison-oak tree.

—William Garvin

"Wow! Did you see the size of that rock he gave her?"

"Say, did you have that broken arm when I left for work this morning?"

Heredity

"My son's intelligence comes from me,"
Bragged Mr. Pompenstine.
His wife remarked, "I quite agree—
Because I've still got mine."

—Joe Wagner

Energy Crisis Solved

The small boy excitedly told his Dad, "Wow! You should see the neat lawn mower the man across the street has. It doesn't need gas, an electric cord or anything to work—all you have to do is push it."

—George Bergman

Life With Son

An optimist is a father who will let his son take the new car on a date. A pessimist is one who won't. A cynic is one who did.

—Lucille S. Harper

From the Pocket

To have loved and lost is much cheaper.

—Walter Schmidt

At Ease

It makes her ill at ease
When the kids want to riot;
But she feels much worse
When they are quiet.

—Homer Phillips

"It looks like an overdose of flashbulbs."

The Truth Fairy

Michele was sobbing. She had a baby tooth pulled the day before, and when she looked under her pillow next morning she discovered the Good Fairy had not left her any tooth money. Her mother said, "You're a big girl now; you don't still believe in fairies, do you?"

"No," Michele replied, "but I still believe in money."

—David Bissonette

So We Did It

At first we all explored it,
And, frankly, I abhorred it.
But the wife and the kids adored it—
Because we couldn't afford it.

—Harold Rowley

"Yes, I know he's going through a stage, but I'm going to try to speed him up a little."

"He never takes anything seriously."

What's Sauce for the Goose Is Gooseberry for the Gosling

You say that I don't look a day
  older than my daughter,
It's kind of you to say so, sir,
  but you hadn't oughter,
I'm pleased as punch you think so,
  and it cheers *me* up no end,
But from the look on my daughter's face,
  I'd say you've lost a friend.

—*Veronica M. Sharer*

Have We Met?

A young man was too timid to ask the man personally for his daughter's hand, so he phoned her father. "Do you care if Jane and I get married?" he asked. "No," replied the father. "Who is calling?"

—*Rose L. Sands*

"No, I wouldn't exactly call Ed God-fearing. It's more like Mabel is God-fearing and Ed fears Mabel."

Same to Ya

Overheard: "My husband is a do-it-yourself man. Every time I ask him to do something, he says, 'Do it yourself.' "

—Herm Albright

Give Him Time

To my friend's disgust, her husband is not a demonstrative person. When newlyweds moved in next door she took the opportunity to give him a not too subtle hint. "He kisses her good-bye in the morning and hello at night," she said. "Why can't you do the same?"

"My dear," he replied mildly, "I only met the woman last week."

—Margaret Shauers

Planned Husbandhood

While other men paint
Or water or weed
I'm curled in a chair
With a good book to read.

While other men shop
Or shovel or mow,
I'm having a beer
While watching some show.

I offer to help,
But my wife says, "Forget it,
If you lend a hand,
I know I'll regret it."

And therein's my secret:
I'm very adept
At only one thing,
And that's being inept.

—F. O. Walsh

Grounds for Marriage

A young man announced to a co-worker that he was getting married.

"I'm sick and tired of eating TV dinners, darning my own socks, making the bed, and going to the laundromat," he said.

"That's funny," declared his crony, "I got divorced for the same reason."

—Honey Greer

"Now all we need are some friends."

Sure Thing

We bought it twenty years ago,
And used it only once, although
We moved the thing from place to place,
And always found it storage space.
So I gave in to my tidy spouse,
And yesterday, while cleaning house,
I let her throw the thing away.
I needed it again today.

—F.O. Walsh

Blood is Thicker?

Not finished dressing for my date, I asked my young brother to keep him company when he came. My brother politely said "Hello" and then added, "Why do you come to see my sister? Don't you have one of your own?"

—George E. Bergman

Acceptable Absence

Employer—"Why do you want to take two weeks off?"

Employee—"I'd like to accompany my bride on her honeymoon."

—Mrs. B. Bader

Stalemate

Father (to daughter's boyfriend): "She'll be right down. Care for a game of chess?"

—Rose Sands

"It's still hard to believe they really meant *the coupon offer was limited one to a family . . . "*

For Starters

"I agree," said the psychiatrist, "that your son may have a spark of genius. But, in my opinion, he also has some ignition trouble."

—Herm Albright

That's the Spirit!

The living room's knee deep
With wrappings in a heap
And every kind of toy and game and doll.
Amid this festive clutter
I hear my children mutter
To each other in a whisper, "Is that all?"

—Jill Halley Walker

"Oh, for heaven's sake, Wesley, don't be absurd! How can I make them stop staring at you?!"

"Wherever one goes, the other goes."

Keeping the Peace

To keep your marriage brimming
With love in the loving cup,
Whenever you're wrong admit it,
Whenever you're right shut up.
—*Rose Sands*

Limited Repertoire

After listening to his eight-year-old son saw away on his violin practice accompanied by the howling of the family dog, the father inquired, "Can't you play something the dog doesn't know?"

—*George Bergman*

"So we decided to make it into a lamp."

Vignette in a Launderette

"Remember," said the old man
To the woman at his side,
"When washing billowed on the line
And you were just a bride?"

"I remember," said the woman,
Putting money in a dryer.
"Remember," said the old man,
"How you tiptoed reaching higher?"

"Then," said he, "the world was sane,
And love and beauty were ordained."
"I remember," said the woman,
"Only that it rained."

—*A. D. Huey*

Turn About

It was snowing heavily and the roads were terribly slick as the family set out on a trip. On a hill the car suddenly made a half-revolution at the center of the road, leaving them facing the direction from which they had come. Everyone was shaking except the slightly deaf grandmother. Instead, she asked wearily, "What on earth have you forgotten this time?"

—Dorothea Kent

Chow Now

Every boy should have a dog
Psychologists have said.
Of course, he needs a mother too,
To see the dog gets fed.

—Lillian Koslover

"Sorry about your image, son, but I'm afraid you're stuck with the same 'creepy old station wagon' that your Mother and I use."

Who Needs Friends?

A college student wired home: "Am without friends and funds."

His father wired back: "Make friends."

—Lucille J. Goodyear

Hot Line

Our daughter, Alicia,
Had just turned sixteen,
And was earning the title
Of "Telephone Queen."

For her birthday we gave her
Her own private phone
Along with instructions
To leave ours alone.

Now we still catch her using
Our line, with the stall,
"I can't tie mine up, Mom,
I might get a call."

—Louella Dunann

silly stuff

Law Abiding

Kitman's Law: Pure drivel tends to drive off the TV screen ordinary drivel.
Sattinger's Law: It works better if you plug it in.
The Law of the Perversity of Nature: You cannot successfully determine beforehand which side of the bread to butter.

—The Peter Prescription

Pastor's Peccadillo

In Boston a minister noticed a group of boys standing around a small, stray dog. "What are you doing, boys?"

"Telling lies," said one of the boys. "The one who tells the biggest lie gets the dog."

"Why, when I was your age," the shocked minister said, "I never even thought of telling a lie."

The boys looked at one another, a little crestfallen. Finally one of them shrugged and said, "I guess he wins the dog."

—Lane Olinghouse

M and M

Manic-depressive: One whose life is easy glum, easy glow.
Middle Age: That time in a man's life when he returns a wink . . . with a blink.

—Lucille J. Goodyear

Current Complaint

In my kitchen nothing's working—
Percolators have stopped perking.
Simple toasters and Mixmasters
In my keeping are disasters,
Also, freezers, blenders, fryers,
Timers, mashers, and clothes dryers.
Other rooms are likewise haunted
With the gadgets I once wanted—
Bargains that turned into boo-boos,
Cuckoo clocks without their cuckoos.
Radio or tape recorder—
If it's mine, it's out of order.
Television? I can't work it,
Nor vibrators that short-circuit.
Where appliances hygienic
Are concerned, I am a cynic.
Toothbrushes, electric, foil me,
Saunas usually parboil me.
Hateful instruments, enslavers—
Heaven save me from *TIME-SAVERS!*

—Frances Barton

Blaze of Glory

The fourth-grade pupil's history paper advised, "It was Nathan Hale who said 'I regret that I have but one life to give for my country' and this has come to be known as Haley's Comment."

—Gloria McCoy

Successful Planning

We go on vacation to forget things and we no sooner get where we planned than we find we did.

—George E. Bergman

Daffynitions

Minibus: Puny express.
Flu Shot: An ouch of prevention.
Orthopedic Specialist: Marrow-minded physician.

—Audrey Earle

"Thank heavens it's Friday!!!"

Occupational Hazard
(School Bus Division)

Third seat left sneaks on his kittens;
The girl beside him loses mittens.
Fifth seat right's a boy who shrieks;
Behind him is a lad that reeks.
Eighth seat left's a girl who sits
Angelically, but spits and spits.
Ninth-seat boys scratch window glass;
The whole back row throws shoes and grass.
Pity the school-bus driver's fate:
Retired, with nerves, at 38.

—*William Garvin*

Arm Twister

Class President: "Congratulate me, teacher. I defeated my opponent in today's election!"
Teacher: "Honestly?"
Class President: "Don't bring that up."

—Elaine Neren

Surprise Package

When a parcel is posted
And then coast-to-coasted;
When it's pitched and it's chucked
And it's caught or it's ducked;
When it's sat on and stepped on
And, like as not, slept on;
When it's batted and booted,
Irreparably fluted,
And it's reached its address—
It's a bit hard to guess
What's beneath string and tape
From the package's shape.

—G. Sterling Leiby

Test of Strength

A traveler hesitated at the airline ticket counter, holding a clothing bag by its hook. "Is this strong enough to go in the baggage compartment, or should I carry it aboard?" he asked the clerk.

The ticket clerk took the bag and slammed it against the counter. "That," he said, "is what it'll get on the way from the terminal. This," he went on, throwing it at the wall, "is what will happen when it's put on the plane. And this," he concluded, stamping on it until it burst open, "is what it'll get when it reaches your destination." He handed the wreckage back to the traveler. "I think to be on the safe side you'd better carry it on."

—Thomas J. French

". . . You, Peabody, are one crummy Puritan!"

Guide to Hospital Personnel For Those Who Feel a Pain Coming On

Neurologist: twitch doctor.
Pathologist: whys man.
Radiologist: X-rayted cameraman.
Nurse: needlepoint expert.
Pediatrician: bawl bouncer.
Gynecologist: ladies' man.
Cardiologist: circulation manager.
Oculist: seecurer.
Obstetrician: labor supervisor.
Podiatrist: corn borer.
Dermatologist: skin dehiver.

—Llewellyn Mitstifer

A Breadful Answer

"Of all the parables," began the Sunday-school teacher, "which do you enjoy the best?"

"I like the one about the multitude that loafs and fishes," came a prompt reply from a young parishioner.

—Michael J. Harman

Hail, Caesar

Immigration officer: "Are you a natural-born citizen?"

"No, I'm a Caesarean."

—Dorothea Kent

Sem-Antics

Popsicle: Dad's weed cutter.
Impair: Two-year-old twin boys.
Melancholy: Large pale orange dog.
Copy: Like a policeman.
Dainty: Beverage in Denmark.
Haggard: Witch's protector.
Germinate: Ludwig had lunch.

—Delaine Helwig

Unobservant

On hearing a crash out front a farmer ran out to the road to see what had happened. On the side of the highway he found a motorist, dazed.

"What happened?" he asked.

"A cow suddenly appeared from out of nowhere," replied the motorist, "and I hit her."

Fearing that it might be one of his, the farmer asked, "Was it a Jersey cow?"

"Frankly, I don't know," muttered the motorist. "I didn't see her license."

—D. G. Watson

Daffy Definition

Prosperity: That period between your last installment and the next down payment.

—Lucille J. Goodyear

Fun Facts

What would you call. . . .
a butcher's dance?
  Meatball
a deer who defies a hunter?
  Fast Buck
feet that burn?
  Hot Dogs
a meeting of sheep?
  Wool Gathering
a secret marriage of two insects?
  Antelope
a small hot dog?
  Teeny Weeny
what animals do in the fall?
  Refer
the trip of a sub?
  Submission
an insect in the garden of Eden?
  Adamant
a horse who keeps late hours?
  Nightmare
a sleeping male cow?
  Bulldozer

—Selma Glasser

Precocious Kid

When asked to define "agriculture," nine-year-old Willie rose nobly to the occasion. "Agriculture," said he, "is something like farming, only farming is doing it!"

—Phil Liechty

Pieces of Eight

The pizza man asked the teenager whether he should cut his pizza in six or eight pieces. The teenager thought a minute before replying: "Better cut it in six pieces, I don't think I can eat eight."

—George Bergman

Sweet Sorrow

Money talks,
And it makes me cry,
For all it says
Is good-bye.

—Ramona Demery

Post Haste

"I want to speak to the postmaster. Right this minute!"

"This is the postmaster speaking, ma'am. What seems to be the trouble?"

"I had to call the Society for the Prevention of Cruelty to Animals, just because of one of your dad-burned mailmen!"

"I'm terribly sorry to hear that, ma'am. What did he do?"

"Well, he's a-sittin' in the tree in my yard and he's got my poor doggie so excited she won't eat!"

Daffy Definitions

Summer Resorts: Places where the prices are double and none of the men are single.
Bank Loan Renewal: Rendezvous with debt.
Surfer: Man overboard.

—Lucille Goodyear

"Corn again?"

Party Pooper

Indignant wife to husband as they leave party: "Just because I'm a few pounds overweight, I wish you'd stop referring to me as a barrel of fun."

—*George E. Bergman*

Something Missing

An absentminded professor drove up to the door of his garage, looked inside, blinked, then backed out of the driveway, drove full speed to the police station, and ran in.

"Sergeant!" he cried. "My car's been stolen!"

—*Bob Pedigo*

"Strangest thing I've ever seen . . . Cronkite said something about the 'lighter side' of the news and burst into tears."

Sem-antics

Locomotive: Crazy reason.
Oversight: 20/20 and then some.
Detergent: Stop that man!
Abate: Fishing lure.

—Delaine Helwig

Afterthought

The first day of school and the teacher told her kindergarten class, "If anyone has to go to the bathroom, he should hold up two fingers."

After a moment of quiet thought, one little boy asked: "How will that help?"

—George E. Bergman

That's About the Size of it

A man walked into a dress shop and told the clerk he wanted to buy a formal evening gown for his wife.

"What," asked the clerk, "are your wife's measurements?"

The man thought for a moment. "Small, medium and large," he declared, "and in that order."

—Honey Greer

De-FUN-itions

State of the Union Message: I do.
British TV station: English Channel.
Prisoner's population count: Consensus.
Stallion's zipper: Horsefly.
Short laugh: Minnehaha.
Hangout for birds: Crowbar.
Two drunks: Pair o' tights.
Bed for youth: Boycott.
Money collected from sinners: Syntax.
Auto song: Cartoon.
Car driven by female: Unmanned vehicle.

—Selma Glasser

Frustrated Poet

I can hear my pallbearers beefing
As they hoist me outa the hearse:
"This son of a gun weighs nearly a ton"
(I'm taking my unpublished verse).

—Jon Slagle

Willing Subject

Fashion: The only form of dictatorship universally accepted.

—R. H. Grenville

Ideal Location

What if national organizations held their annual conventions in the following cities?
Weight Watchers—Gainesville, Fla.
Society of American Surgeons—Lansing, Mich.
Certified Dental Hygienists—Ivory Coast, W. Africa
National Contortionist's League—South Bend, Ind.
Voyeurs Unlimited—Peking, China
Xerox Corporation—Walla Walla, Wash.
American Institute of Urology—Niagara Falls, N.Y.
7-UP—Pensacola, Fla.
National Organization of Plumbers—Flushing, N.Y.

—Sheila R. Schultz

Overheard

Some things you just have to tell in confidence; otherwise no one would listen.

—Julius Spring

Stocking up for New Year's

The Chinese believe in settling all their year's debts before New Year's. However, they do not have Christmas the week before.

—George E. Bergman

Webster Never Defined 'em Like This

Maternity ward: An heirport.
Waiter: A person who can dish it out but can't bake it.
Claustrophobia: A fear of Santa Claus.
Toupee: A bareskin rug.
Drunkenness: The shortest distance between two pints.
Birth control pill: A laborsaving device.
Bankruptcy: A fate worse than debt.

—John Murtaugh

"What else do you have to declare . . . ?"

Politician

Politician: The only person who can throw his hat in the ring and continue to talk through it.

—Ed Dussault

Intimations of Immorality

For a Creative Writing class at the University of Chicago, an aspiring young woman submitted (as young females often do) a story about a young woman. At one point in the narrative, her heroine ". . . tripped, tumbled the full length of the stair, and lay prostitute at the bottom." The graduate assistant who helped the professor with grading was at a loss how to comment on the heroine's extremely awkward position. He marked the word and handed the manuscript across the table to the professor, who solemnly read the questionable passage, equally solemnly wrote something in the margin, and passed it back.

Eager to learn the master's teaching techniques, the

assistant read the marginal note: "My dear young lady, if you hope ever to become a writer, you must immediately learn to distinguish between a fallen woman and one who has only stumbled."

—Shea Lebed

Mirror—Thy Sting is Heartless

Toupee, or not toupee? That is the question:
Whether 'tis nobler in the mind to suffer
The comb and scissors of outrageous barbers,
Or to take arms against the wispy remainders,
And, by shaving, end them—to cut—to snip
No more—and, by a wig, to say we end
The heartache, and the thousand shocks
That scalp is heir to—'tis a consummation
Devoutly to be wished. To dye—to slick—
To slick! Perchance, to comb—ay, there's the rub;
For in that run of comb through hair what dreams may
  come,
When we have muffled off our shiny dome,
Must give us pause.

—Robert E. Tinsley

"You mean this isn't *45 Oak St.?"*

Love Note

A girl about twelve years old handed a check to a bank teller.

"You'll have to endorse it," said the teller as he returned the check.

"What does endorse mean?" asked the little girl.

"Just sign your name like you do in a letter," explained the teller.

Smiling shyly the girl wrote, "Love, Linda."

—Lillian Koslover

Daffynition

Decathlon Contestant: Jock of all trades.

—Gloria Rosenthal

Into the Frying Pan

A teacher was trying to explain the difference between involvement and commitment, but his students couldn't seem to understand. He finally got through to them when he said, "Let us consider a breakfast of ham and eggs. In a ham and egg breakfast, the chicken is involved, but it is the pig who is committed."

—Susan Baumgartner

business as usual

Showing No Quarter

Uncle Bill, a very frugal and cautious old man, put on his best clothes and went to the city one day. As he was standing on a street corner, a shabby stranger approached and asked, "Will you give me a quarter for a sandwich?"

Uncle Bill gave him a good looking over, then said, "Lemme see the sandwich first."

—Lucille S. Harper

Can't You Read?

For many months, the salesman had eaten at a diner that advertised "Martha's Home Cooking," but he had never seen Martha. One day, he approached the counterman and said, "This is a good place to eat, and I always enjoy my meals here, but I never see Martha. Where is she?"

"Where the sign says she is," was the reply. "Home cooking."

—Samuel J. Stannard

"As far as management's concerned, Mrs. Johnson, it's your responsibility to take the suit off your husband before you bring it in for cleaning."

How To Increase Property Value

The first man to make a mountain out of a molehill was probably a real estate dealer.

—Lucille S. Harper

Catch a Husband

The business tycoon's daughter was on vacation from college and he was showing her around the newly acquired family estate. They stopped at the oversized swimming pool to watch several athletic and handsome young men perform from the diving board.

"Oh, Daddy!" exclaimed the daughter. "You've stocked it for me!"

—G. L. Boyce

Spaced Out

Then there was the new young secretary who asked her boss if he also wanted the carbon copies double spaced.

—George E. Bergman

Philosopher

"Money is not too important,
Not nearly as precious as health.
Happiness, Home, Reputation,
All rate far ahead of mere wealth.
Be grateful for life's simple pleasures,
Avoiding the wealth-seeking craze,
For money is not too important,"
Said the boss when I asked for a raise.

—Harry Lazarus

"I'm sure glad I don't have to run a business under some of these laws we've passed!"

Installment Trying

Pete and his wife were looking at furniture. "For this sofa," exclaimed the salesman, "you make a small down payment, then you make no more payments for six months. . . ."

Suddenly Pete grabbed his wife's arm and hurried her out of the store. "Drat it," he muttered as they trotted up the sidewalk, "someone's sending ahead warnings about us."

—Penny Lindsay Allison

"Walters, you make potholes; Allan, you make bumps; and Bufkin, you crumble the road edges."

"And I assure you the continued existence of mankind is high on my list of priorities."

Consumer's Retort

A nomad returned to the Arabian desert after a trip to the United States. As he unpacked, his friends asked him what had impressed him the most there. "Was it the tall buildings?" asked one. When he replied in the negative he was asked, "What, then?"

"American salesmen," he replied as he very carefully unwrapped an outboard motor.

—*G. G. Crabtree*

We Aren't Getting Younger

The expert asked the personnel director, "How many employees do you have approaching retirement?"

The personnel director eyed the efficiency expert thoughtfully, then replied mildly, "Well, we haven't any employees going the other way."

—*Rich Rollins*

I assure you, Gentlemen, it's just a matter of days before management and the girls get together on a new contract . . .

Youthful Approach

Friend to salesman: "To what do you owe your success?" Salesman: "To the first five words I utter when a woman opens the door: 'Miss, is your mother in?' "

—Herm Albright

Presidential Caliber

The young man had been on the job for several months and still seemed to be doing everything wrong.

One day his supervisor came over and in a fatherly manner put his hand on the young man's shoulder. "Did you know," he said in sympathy, "that you and the president of this firm have something in common?"

"Really?" beamed the young man. "And what is it?"

"Both of you have climbed about as far as you can go in this company!"

—Tom Kovach

Oops!

A businessman attending a convention sent his wife a telegram that contained an unfortunate typographical error. "Having a wonderful time," it read. "Wish you were her."

—Lane Olinghouse

At Home with a Cold

Of all the sniffles, pains, and aches
With which the common cold can clout us,
Nothing is more distressing than
Seeing how well things run without us.

—Walt Streightiff

Vaulting Ambition

"How come you lost your job?" questioned the clerk at the unemployment office.

"The foreman was jealous."

"Jealous! Of what?"

"Well, you know what a foreman does," the young worker began to explain, "just stands around and watches people."

"Yes."

"Too many people thought I was the foreman."

—Michael Harman

Low Sales Diet

"Are you on a diet?" asked the salesman's friend, when he saw him eating milk and crackers. "No," was the reply. "On commission."

—Herm Albright

How to Lower Your Interest Rates

If you don't want to worry
About Truth-In-Lending,
Make sure you earn more
Than you are spending.

—Anton F. Gross

"I told you, Eunice—Federal regulations require a substantial penalty in case of early withdrawal."

"Did you hear about poor Ralph? He got laid off!"

Efficiency Check

Note in Mary's paycheck envelope: "Your increase in salary will become effective as soon as you do."

—Lucille S. Harper

Payroll Parley

A worker opened his pay envelope to discover the payroll department had shorted him one dollar. Angrily, he complained to the cashier about the discrepancy.

The cashier patiently looked through the records, then said: "Last week we overpaid you a dollar. Why didn't you complain about that mistake?"

The worker drew himself up to full height. "An occasional mistake I can overlook," he replied. "But not two in a row."

—Lane Olinghouse

"Make sure this is not leaked to the press until Lieutenant Cooper's had an opportunity to correct my spelling."

Leaves From Our Own Yellowed Pages

A selection of business enterprises culled from
a wholly imaginary directory:
Changing Times Diaper Service
Conclusion Jumper Co.
Couth or Consequences School of Etiquette
Goldie Lox and the Three Bagels Deli
Hammond Eggs
Helfer Leather Co.
Mutton Jeff Butcher Shop
Sketch-as-Sketch-Can Art School
Suture Self Surgical Equipment
Thick and Thin Adhesives
Upson-Downes Elevator Co.
Wilde & Wooley Underwear

—Edward Stevenson

Slightly Overslept . . .

Jim was having problems getting up in the morning, so his doctor prescribed some pills. Jim took them, slept well, and was awake before he heard the alarm.

He took his time getting to the office, strolled in and said to the boss: "I didn't have a bit of trouble getting up this morning."

"That's fine," replied his boss. "But where were you yesterday?"

—Lucille Goodyear

The Real Owner

Real estate taxes are a method that allows you to buy a house, then rent it back from the city every year.

—Anonymous

"Harkins has devised a terrific new sales angle—we make our product reliable, durable, and economical."

Anti-diluvian

The young lawyer was very anxious to make a good impression in presenting his first case. He started out by saying:

"Long ago, before the world was even created——"

Before he could go on, the judge interrupted:

"Mr. Burton," he intoned, "we have other cases to try and we're very busy today. Would you mind starting at least after the flood?"

—Lloyd Byers

"Oh, Yeah? Opportunity who?"

The Price of Labor

The machine in the large factory stopped working and everything came to a grinding halt. A repairman was called in. He merely tapped the machine with a hammer and it began working again. When he submitted a bill for $250, the plant manager felt the charge was too high for a little tap of the hammer, and demanded an itemized bill. The repairman complied with the request and sent a second bill. It specified:
Tapping with hammer—$50.00
Knowing where to tap—$200.00

—Rose Sands

Virtue Unrewarded

I'm weary of people
Who brag and who boast
That early risers
Accomplish the most.

I'm tired of hearing
That story, absurd,
About the success
Of the early bird.

The people who quote it
Forget, as folks do,
The fact that the worm
Got up early, too.

—Anne McCarroll

Promising Future

The vocational counselor told the young applicant: "Your vocational aptitude test indicates that your best opportunities exist wherever your father holds an influential position."

—Lucille J. Goodyear

Don't Bank on It

There was a time when a man who saved money was considered a miser. These days he's a genius.

—*Audrey Earle*

Busy, Busy, Busy Day!

I've gone for a drink and sharpened my pencils,
Searched through my desk for forgotten utensils,
Reset my watch and adjusted my chair,
Loosened my tie and straightened my hair,
Emptied the wastebasket, filled the carafe,
Sorted the paper clips, opened the safe,
Filled my pen and tested the blotter,
Gone for another drink of water,
Adjusted the calendar, raised the blinds,
Sorted erasers of different kinds.
Now, down to work I can finally sit.
Oops! Too late. It's time to quit!

—*Leonard A. Paris*

"I think you've just written the great American memo!!"

"Bring him down a peg or two, Roger! Tell him how many times you could buy and sell him!"

No Window Dressing

The customer approached the clothing store salesman and said, "I would like to try on that suit in the window."

Salesman: "I'm sorry, sir. You'll have to use the dressing room."

—*George Bergman*

"It says, 'I've decided to take it all with me, even the lawyer's fee.' "

Hoarse and Buggy

An overworked executive came down with a severe summer cold. First his voice became slightly hoarse, then extremely hoarse. Finally it gave out entirely. To show he had not lost his sense of humor, he placed a sign on his desk that read, "Sorry, folks. Sound is out."

One of his associates, after regarding his miserable and haggard look, placed a second sign beside the first: "Picture is terrible, too."

—Lane Olinghouse

Thrown for a Loss

A department store was in the midst of its annual sale on yard goods. There was quite a crowd with everyone shoving and pushing around the table where there was a ten-yard limit on some fine material. A rather irate woman, completely disheveled, complained to the manager that she had been shoved out of line by another woman.

The manager pointed a finger at the offending party, and instructed the salesgirl, "Penalize that lady five yards!"

—Honey Greer

The Little Shop Around the Corner

Quiggensby, Higgins & Briggs
Are dealers in thingumajigs,
With a stock of all sorts
From secondhand warts
To dandruff removers for wigs.

—Hal Chadwick

"Just how long is 'all the live long day'?"

"Hold it a moment, Burston! I smell money!"

A Puzzling Response

The personnel manager asked the young job applicant if she had any special qualifications or unusual talents. "Yes, sir," she said. "Last year I won several prizes in crossword puzzle and slogan-writing contests."

The manager smiled. "That sounds good—but we need people who are smart during office hours."

"Oh," the girl responded hastily, "this was during office hours."

—Lane Olinghouse

Taking Stock

A man who had bumped his head and gone into a coma awoke clearheaded and refreshed in 1996. The first thing he did was to phone his broker who informed him that his AT&T stock was now worth $5 million, his GM stock $10 million, and his Xerox stock $15 million. "Golly," the man exclaimed excitedly, "I'm rich!" Then the phone operator interrupted him. "Your three minutes are up. Deposit $1 million please."

—Dorothea Kent

In Father's Footsteps

Students at a local high school were asked to tell their big ambition in life. One young man explained: "I have dreams of making a million dollars in show business just like my father."

The teacher asked, "Did your father really make a million dollars in show business?"

"No, he didn't," declared the student. "But he had dreams, too."

—Honey Greer

"It's very well done . . . but we feel there's just no market for a cleaned-up version of the Bible."

Easily Satisfied

Employer: "I'm sorry, but we can't hire you. We just don't have enough work to keep you busy."

Applicant: "It really takes surprisingly little."

—Samuel Stannard

Perpetual Payments

My stack of bills
Has me perplexed and beset,
By the question
Of a life after debt.

—Gail Cooke

Paperclips

Many a boss blows off steam at the office because he's in hot water at home.

Seeing how some people hold their liquor is enough to suggest that the original container held it better.

—Hal Chadwick

yours truly

It's Friends Like That . . .

Dear Helen,

I had to go out on an errand so if you come while I'm gone, go on in and get the pressure cooker. (You know where the key is.) Talk to you later.

Marian

Dear Marian,

Guess I missed you but I did get the pressure cooker. I couldn't find the key at first; you must not keep it buried by the tulips anymore. I finally found it over by the ivy and listen, don't worry, you can get that ivy back to looking great in no time. But you know I couldn't get that key to work somehow and I had to pry your basement window open. The screwdriver I was using slipped and broke that one pane. I finally got in and I just couldn't remember where you kept your pressure cooker so I had to search for it. I really didn't have time to put all that stuff away so hope you won't mind doing that when you get back. I guess the cat followed me in and when I was down on my knees looking in that lower cupboard she must have crawled in. It was when I was trying to pull her out that the flour spilled on the floor. When I was looking for her later on to put her out I noticed those white footprints on your couch. At least it was easier to find her that way. Ha! Anyway, I got her back out as I knew you wouldn't want her inside getting into things while you were gone. Thanks for the loan, Marian, and I'll see you tonight at bridge club. It is at your house this time, isn't it?

See you then.

Helen

—*Patricia Wentworth*

"For the twentieth time, Rahotep: before except after or when sounded like as in neighbor and weigh."

Misguided Missive

15 January, 1490

Dear Queen Isabella:

As a loyal subject I feel impelled to warn you about a man named Columbus. He is planning to come to you with an elaborate scheme for exploring the oceans. Please do not be taken in by him. He has a fatal flaw in his makeup which I will tell you about.

I met this man in a public house in Lisbon. He was moving from table to table pleading for someone to buy him a glass of port. When he came to my table I was intrigued by the mad glint in his eye, and invited him to drink with me.

In short order he was confiding in me. He told me that he was an experienced sailor with but one severe drawback: lack of a sense of direction. He said he frequently gets lost finding his way home, only two squares from the tavern. Once he set out from his hometown of Genoa for Corsica and landed in Portuguese Africa, discovering five or six new islands on the way. But he never could tell anyone how to find them again.

Like many navigators today, he believes there are islands to the west yet untouched by civilization. He plans to ask you for financial help in outfitting three ships to find these islands for the glory of Spain. I beseech you to resist his pleadings. Tell him to go back to buying sugar for Genoese merchants. And send him home. Or tell him to get lost. Which he will have no trouble doing.

Loyally,
Loyalle y Loyalles

cc: King Ferdinand

—Mort Singer

Full Steam Ahead

All the letters I write
  Make me feel such a sap,
I remember all the important things
  After I've sealed the flap!

—Carroll S. Karch

"On second thought, let's just change that to, 'Dear Sir'."

"Which do you think sounds better, Miss Hutton, 'All the problems of the world would be solved if people only understood each other', or, 'All the problems of the world would be solved if people would only stop trying to understand each other'?"

Diary of a Dinner

October 6, 1974

Dear Peg and Tom,

Bert and I are planning a dinner for twelve on Saturday, October 22, at 7:30 p.m. Cocktails will be served an hour earlier. We certainly hope you'll be able to attend. Please drop us a line and let us know if we may expect you.

Sincerely,
Jean

October 10, 1974

Dear Jean,

Thank you so much for your dinner invitation. We were delighted. Your dinners are always such fun and we certainly are looking forward to it.

My mother will be away that particular weekend and will be unable to baby-sit for us. It seems such a shame to hire a sitter when all four children are so used to their grandmother. They're very little trouble so we've decided to just take them with us.

Would you mind very much setting up your old crib somewhere as Chris is too young to sleep in a bed for the evening? Peggy Jane and Kenny will watch their favorite TV shows so you'll hardly notice them there. Peggy Jane is nearly trained and they rarely fight anymore. Maureen prefers reading, so a pile of books and a few snacks will keep her entertained. Perhaps one of your older girls could stay in the room with Chris as he sometimes attempts to climb out of the crib. He's getting so cute and so inquisitive.

I do hope you intend to serve that nice white wine we enjoyed at your last dinner. It was so tasty for a domestic wine and so much cheaper than the imports. Tom said the canapes bothered his stomach most of the evening, but I enjoyed them. He's being so careful—mostly eating chicken and bland foods now. Please don't go to any extra fuss—a small casserole for him will be fine. I can eat whatever you intend to serve but must be careful of my salt intake, and please, very little spice or sauce.

We'll see you on the 22nd. It sounds delightful.

As always,
Peg

October 14, 1974

Dear Peg and Tom,

I'm sorry to say that we must cancel the dinner we had planned for the 22nd. Bert must leave on a most unexpected business trip to the Belgian Congo. I've decided to go along with him as it gets so lonesome with only the natives to talk to.

We must get together soon again. I'll be in touch.

As ever,
Jean

—Peggy McGettigan

to your health

Sober Solution

"I just can't find a cause for your illness," the physician said. "To be perfectly frank, I think it's due to drinking."

"In that case," declared the patient, "I'll return when you're sober."

—Honey Greer

Baby Me

While working in the maternity ward, a student nurse asked a young medical student why he was so enthusiastic about obstetrics. He said sheepishly, "When I was on medical rotation I suffered from heart attack, asthma, and itch. In surgery I was sure I had ulcers. In the psychiatric ward I thought I was losing my mind. Now in obstetrics I can relax."

—Dorothea Kent

"You were a riot!"

Take Two Screams, and Call Me in the Morning

"Express your emotions,"
Most doctors say—
"You'll avoid ulcers
And headaches that way."

So, when I am angry,
I slam doors and yell.
I'M FINE!
(But my family's
Not feeling too well.)

—*Anne Komorny*

Belle Boy

The wife of a struggling intern was the belle of the hospital ball. All the men at the party raced each other to dance with her.

"She's quite lovely," he overheard the other wives saying, "but that gown must have cost an arm and a leg."

"Not an arm and a leg," interjected the young doctor sadly. "Eight deliveries, eleven tonsillectomies, and sixty-three flu shots."

—Doris Clarke

Growth Slippage

The fates are, oftentimes, unkind:
We work, to "get ahead" . . .
And then, in middle age, we find
We've got "behind," instead.

—Fred S. Buschmeyer, Jr.

"I'd say offhand he has a fever!"

Mirror, Mirror on the Wall

Oh, mirror, mirror, on the wall,
I look at you and want to bawl.
Where hair once showed a youthful bloom,
A barren dome bespeaks my gloom.
The eyes that gave each conquest birth
Are caught in webs of crow's-feet girth.
The nose, once firm and trim of line,
Now perches there—a bulbous sign.
The chin and cheeks, such noble parts,
Are jellied rolls—no ends, no starts.
The mouth that smiled through thick and thin—
Alas, takes urging—just to grin.
If you weren't such an honest bloke—
I'd punch your face 'til it was broke!

—*R. Lewis*

"No, I thought you *put him in!"*

"First the good news, I'm glad you came to see me, now the bad news, you came too late!"

This "B" is not a Vitamin

The "B" period is what it is called,
The time when you begin to be Bald;
When Bridgework begins to put its bite
Into that which once was life's delight;
When you have a Bulge where you were flat,
And Bifocals tell you where you're at.

—Mildred N. Hoyer

Mounting Vertigo

"Doctor, why is it that when I go down to the cellar, I feel all right, but when I come back up, I feel dizzy?"

The doctor eyed him warily. "That depends. What do you keep in the cellar?"

—Lucille Harper

"As long as this is just a placebo, would you mind prescribing a cheaper brand?"

The Doctor Is Out

Dearest Doctor,

The nurse said that you would be a little late but that I could wait if I wanted to. With a husband home sick with end-of-the-season football depression, one daughter home from school with cold teeth, a poodle in heat, and the Roto Rooter man coming any minute, what else do I have to do?

For one-half hour I sat here rehearsing my symptoms so I wouldn't waste your time with unnecessary details. The next half hour I sat here with a thermometer in my mouth.

Getting a little restless, I decided to straighten your painting of Florence Nightingale standing beside the Hippocratic Oath (or is that Hypocritic?), empty your ashtrays, throw out last year's magazines, water your artificial rhododendron, and take phone messages while your secretary went to the hairdresser.

Two hours have passed. I can't remember why I came, but it must have been pretty bad for me to wait this long.

I think I'll take two aspirins and go to bed. If I wake up in the morning, I'll give you a call.

Your Patient Patient,
Amanda L.

P.S. Your bill is on the desk.

—Alice B. Odom

Weighty Paradox

When I try to explain the dieting game
My answers seem sort of confusing.
When you're battling the bulge
In order to win
You've always got to be losing.

—M. B. Immel

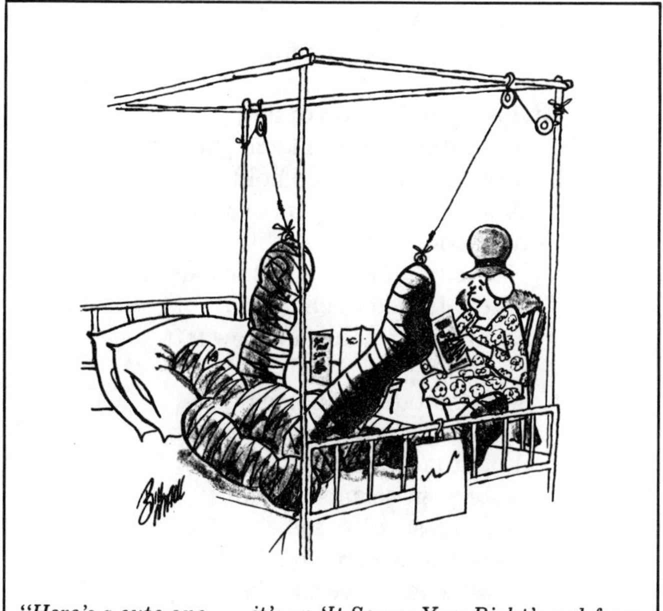

"Here's a cute one . . . it's an 'It Serves You Right' card from the Adams' Roofing Company."

"Ready for seconds?"

**Help Yourself
to the Vitamins**

At dinner in the days of old,
  We simply used to sit and grapple
All a hungry man could hold
  Of beef or bacon, ham or scrapple.
Craving coming from within
  Was all that ever seemed to matter—
Thins continued to be thin;
  Complacently the fats grew fatter.

Now, our modern kitchen queens
  Feed us, mixed and in rotation,
Carbohydrates, starches, greens,
  Proteins in balanced ration.
With a retrospective sigh
  I view the present and decry it—
Once we used to live and die;
  Now we have to live and diet!

—W. B. France

Quick Cure

A hospital visitor approached the floor nurse. "I came to see my friend, Mary Smith. How's she getting along?"

"Very well," smiled the nurse. "Ms. Smith is convalescing now."

"I see," said the visitor. "Well, I'll just wait in the lobby until she's through."

—*Rose Sands*

"My gosh, that's the worst ingrown toenail I've seen!"

"Your symptoms sound like something that's out of my line. Now, there's a specialist at the Johnsons' party down the street."

Diagnosis . . .

A hypochondriac
I don't condone.
He won't leave well enough
Alone.

—*R. Walsh*

Fire! Fire!

A member of the local syndicate, recuperating from a gunshot wound, was wheelchairing down the hospital corridor when a fire extinguisher accidentally fell from its place on the wall and narrowly missed the wheelchair and its occupant. Thinking it was another attack by the hit man, the gangster started screaming for help and went wheeling down the corridor with all his might. A couple of orderlies, thinking the patient had gone berserk, took out after him. A passing nurse, who had snatched up the fallen fire extinguisher, decided that the patient had priority over hospital equipment, and not knowing if it was safe to toss aside the extinguisher, hung on to it and joined the chase.

The procession careened around a turn and almost ran down two elderly ladies on their way to visit sick friends.

Recovering from their sudden fright, the two stared after the fast-moving entourage.

"Now that's what I call fun!" exclaimed one of the old ladies, her eyes twinkling. "Outracing everybody in a wheelchair, yet!"

"That poor man isn't racing for fun, Sarah," the other said, awestruck. "Didn't you see the size of that needle the nurse was aiming at him?"

—William H. Walton

"Exactly how contagious is this, Doctor?"

"It's partly glandular and partly 8,500 calories per day."

Route of the Problem

Delicious foods may make us drool,
But savvy folks observe this rule:
A moment's pleasure on the lips
Can mean a lifetime on the hips.

—*Rosemarie Williamson*

New Contacts

"Dear Doctor," wrote the patient's wife. "My husband used to be a contented, happy family man, an ideal mate and father. Since consulting you, he has become restless, flirtatious, critical of my housekeeping and our children, an ogre about bills, vain, arrogant and, I suspect, a woman-chaser. It is my belief you have been giving him hormone shots which have entirely changed his personality. My next appeal will be to the medical society."

"Dear Mrs. Jones," came the reply. "In response to

your letter, I have not been giving your husband shots of any kind. I had him fitted with contact lenses."

—Al Lindop

Advertising Age

The old gentleman was being interviewed on his hundredth birthday and was asked what he attributed his good health to. "I can't tell you yet," he advised them. "I'm dickering with two or three TV commercials."

—George E. Bergman

"I'm putting you on monogamy."

End in Sight

The young student nurse was about to begin her first day in a hospital. Remembering the advice of the head nurse, she had resolved to encourage patients. Seeing an elderly man who was sitting up in bed, she greeted him cheerfully and said, "Well, you don't look like you'll be with us much longer."

—*Anne Dirkman*

Delayed Reaction

In the dentist's chair
I was brave and bold
As, in order, he
Drilled me . . .
Filled me.
But moments later,
My blood ran cold:
The amount that he
Billed me
Chilled me!

—*Fred S. Buschmeyer, Jr.*

that's life

Unscheduled Flight

On skis, I leaped into the air,
I came to earth I know not where,
For while I soared so wild—so free,
My flight plan led me to a tree.

—H. B. McCauley

Sneaky Pete

The first words of the Reverend Peterson on a sunny Sunday morning were:

"Friends, the subject of my sermon today is liars and lying. Before I start I want to see the hands of all among you who have read the 18th Chapter of Mark." Almost all the hands were raised.

"You folks," the Reverend continued, "are the very ones I want to talk to, partly because I am your preacher, but mainly because there isn't any such chapter."

—Lloyd Byers

What Else?

Want ad: Lost, billfold—will finder please return hard-to-replace contents such as driver's license; also items with pictures of Washington, Jefferson, Jackson, and Lincoln.

—Rose Sands

The Wet Look

I trusted the weatherman today
And this is all I have to say:
My hair is limp, my clothes are dowdy
From splashing through puddles of "partly cloudy."

—Jean Conder Soule

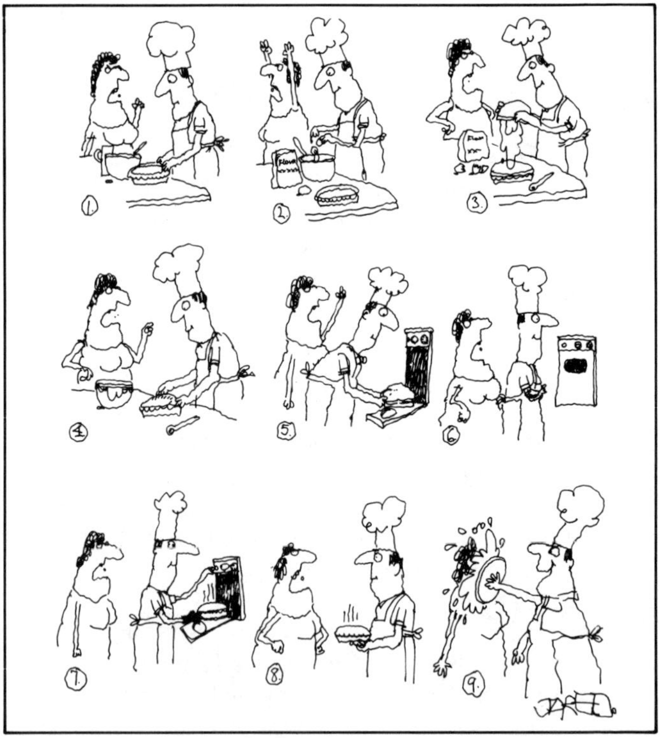

"One thing I can't stand is an actor who thinks he can write!"

Clock Shock

All errands squared away on time
(*Ahead* of time!), my clock
Sounds merry as a nursery rhyme,
And, taking tidy stock,
I (quickly!) tackle "one more thing"
Before I leave . . . and then
Just guess whose phone begins to ring,
And—oops—I'm LATE again!

—Maureen Cannon

Curbing One's Curiosity

The man was lying in the gutter listening to a curb. A policeman walked over and asked him what he was listening to. The man said, "Come on down here and listen."

The policeman got on his hands and knees, then got right back up and said, "I can't hear anything!"

"That's the way it's been all day," replied the man.

—Lucille S. Harper

"If you ask me, the more aid to education we vote, the harder we're making it on future politicians."

The Bright Side

There are none more optimistic
Than the reassuring crowds
Who point out silver linings
In other people's clouds.

—*Suzanne Douglas*

How To Succeed

He was young and ambitious. His job at the small Midwestern radio station entitled him to spin records, give wire service news and weather reports, announce local farm and church events, and sweep the floor.

As he entered the studio early one morning he heard the click-clack-clack of the wire services receiver. He read the slowly emerging print-out. It was a report of the assassination of Marien Ngouabi, Congo President.

He knew this was an important piece of news which should go on the air immediately. He also knew that he could not possibly pronounce the name correctly.

Thinking quickly, he opened the mike and said, "We have just received word of the assassination of the Congo President. His name is being withheld pending notification of his family."

—Tybie Moshinsky

Why the Ocean Heaves

The gunk that we dump in our ocean
The seas no longer can hide.
What washes up on our beaches
Just isn't fit to be tide.

—Em Johnson

Open Season

Some brand-new members of a hunting club were coming in from their first day's shooting. Since all were unused to handling guns, the casualty list was rather formidable. One had his hand in a sling. One was hopping on one foot. A third looked like the drummer boy in the Revolutionary War picture. "Cheer up," an old member urged. "Judging by the bulge in that bag, you're not coming in empty-handed." "That," said the bag carrier, "is our hunting dog."

—*Dorothea Kent*

"Not only that, but George is no longer an atheist."

"Do you know what we need around here? A take-charge guy."

Unexpected Guests

I didn't mind at first,
When they arrived, though uninvited.
I was, I thought, most gracious,
(Though I scarcely felt delighted).

I tried to make them welcome—
Took them everywhere I went.
But now my hospitality
And patience, both are spent.

So I must try to find a way
Somehow, to let them know:
I've finally decided,
Those five pounds have GOT to go!

—Annie Komorny

Clock Watchers

An elevator operator complained that he was getting tired of people asking him for the time. A friend suggested that he hang a clock in his elevator.

A few weeks later, the friend inquired as to how things were going. "Just awful," declared the elevator operator. "Now, all day long, people ask me, 'Is that clock right?' "

—Honey Greer

Ungentle Oriental

The night we dined out Chinese-style
Our waiter stumbled in the aisle
And showered us with mushroom soup;
It took an hour to regroup.
"Chop suey next," we made it plain;
We cooled our heels; he brought chow mein.
The subgum, though, took just a minute;
I noted that his thumb was in it.
When, last, he poured the scalding tea
Upon my wrist, it came to me:
"Why, all of this—from soup to scorcher—
Must be the Chinese *waiter* torture!"

—Robert Brault

Tee Caddy

At the dinner table, the wife of the inveterate golfer said: "Junior told me that he caddied for you this morning."

"That's it!" exclaimed the golf addict. "I knew I'd seen that kid somewhere before!"

—Audrey Earle

Drop in the Ocean

Two men were discussing their status in life.

"I started out on the theory that the world had an opening for me," one man said.

"And have you found it?" the other asked.

"Well, yes," replied the first. "I'm in the hole now."

—Bernadette Dirkman

Mute Point

Silence, it has been divined,
Can greatly aid your peace of mind,

Unless it falls like crack of doom,
Just when you walk into the room.

—F. E. Bartlett

"That's exactly what he said . . . 'Immediate seating on all floors'! . . . "

Inflation . . .

A man had posted himself in front of an office building with a tray of shoelaces. One executive made it a daily habit to give the unfortunate man a dime, but he never took the laces.

One day the peddler, on receiving the dime, tapped his departing benefactor on the back. "I don't like to complain, sir—but the laces are now twenty cents."

—Lucille J. Goodyear

The Tee of Bitterness

I swung and missed yet another time,
The team gave a mighty groan.
I fumbled a pass—the bleachers howled
As I fractured my collarbone.
I dropped the torch near the race's end,
and heard the spectators moan.
But the day I made that hole in one
I was playing a round alone!

—Eileen M. Bunk

"Did I get him?"

"A bit unorthodox in his training methods perhaps . . . but he wins meets."

Guess What's on Your Nose, Dear

The dumbest insect in the world they say's
  the common fly.
His brain is truly tiny and his I.Q. isn't high.
But stupid though the fly may be,
He never fails to outwit me,
For, every time I hear one buzz,
I swat not where he's *at*, but *was*!

—Addison H. Hallock

Compromise

They say it is better to be poor and happy than rich and miserable. But couldn't something be worked out, such as being moderately rich and just moody?

—*Augusta, Kansas,* Gazette

"It's really potatoes."

Misnomer:
The Income Tax Return

Whoever named this federal form
Was lacking in discern;
For how can so much going out
Be labeled a "return"!

—Lillian Dorian

What a Year

A woman returned home after a visit next door, and remarked to her husband: "Mrs. Jones just told me the city council voted Mr. Jones Man-of-the-Year."

The woman's husband shrugged. "That just shows you," he said, "what kind of a year it's been."

—Lane Olinghouse

Knocking the Truth

"Can you describe your assailant?" the officer asked as he helped the bruised man up from the pavement.

"That," said the man, "is just what I was doing when he hit me."

—Anne Dirkman

Education

I push, I pull, I poke and pry;
I break a nail and almost cry.
I finally tear the paper sheath
And dig into the box beneath.

With this upended, then I see
The contents roll out merrily;
And on the bottom (?) plain and clear,
In bold, black letters: OPEN HERE!

—Tedi White

"I've listed two. One for her overall charisma and one I'd personally enjoy."

Post Toast

As you slide down the banister of life, may all the splinters be pointed in the right direction.

—Kemmons Wilson

Vehicles for Revenge

It's far too late for him I hate;
His wrong he can't redress.
Whatever fate I predicate,
I shall be pitiless.

I'll kick that clown all over town,
Which won't reduce my rancor.
I'll weight him down and watch him drown,
And use him for an anchor.

His bod may boil in bubbling oil,
Or writhe upon the rack.
And though it's croil I shan't recoil:
I'll tie him to the track.

A wicked blow may work him woe;
So may a nasty knife.
Or a la Poe I'll stow my foe
Behind a wall for life.

What injury did he to me
That I should be so graphic?
Of treachery the apogee—
He cut me off in traffic.

—James Whiting

Negative Personalities

Some people are like blotters: they soak up everything and get it all backwards.

—Lucille Harper

"Give me an A."

Ye of Little Faith

A man who liked to hike over all kinds of terrain fell over a cliff one day but managed to grab a strong branch. Although his arm and shoulder pained, he held on desperately. He looked down a thousand feet and up fifty feet. No help in either direction. There was nothing to do but yell and hope someone would hear.

"Is anyone up there?"

"Yes, I am here," was the reply.

"Who are you?"

"I am the Lord. Do you need help?"

"I need it badly and at once."

"Do you have faith?"

"I have all the faith in the world."

"Then let go of that branch."

There was a long pause. Then the hiker called, "Is anyone else up there?"

—John A. Johnston

"There it is Ralph, the high point *of our day."*

"Give him one of these pills every four hours, then use this to stop your bleeding."

Speak to Me With Love

Some people talk to plants, you know,
Endearing words to make them grow.
The plants respond and really thrive,
They're just so glad to be alive.
It's such a lovely theory
That I hesitate to query,
But after all the nasty things I've said,
Why don't those hateful weeds drop dead?

—Elise J. Farrow

No Heap

A tourist in New Mexico struck up a conversation with a native father and son. After a while, he squinted up at the blazing sky, licked his dry lips and said, "I do kinda wish it would rain, don't you?" "Yeah," came the reply, "but more for my boy's sake than mine. I've seen it rain."

—Anonymous

Era of Change

I found an open metered space!
 I nearly died of shock!
Yet there it was—a vacant place
 And in the perfect block!
I hadn't had such luck, you see,
 In years beyond recall—
And that's when it occurred to me:
 I had no change at all!

—Dick Emmons

Dead Ahead

Another place that seems to arrive almost before you get started is the bridge that you were going to cross when you got to it.

—Colusa, California, Sun-Herald

Bared

Bore: "That rug on the floor is from a bear I shot in the wilds out west. It was a case of him or me."

Bored: "Have to admit—the bear certainly makes a better rug."

—George Bergman

Be My Pest

Mindful of my cat's delight
In visiting his friends by night,
I made a two-way door that he
Could use without disturbing me.
Uneasy still I lie abed—
His cronies visit him instead.

—Philip Nicholson

"He wasn't actually skiing at the time. He was only trying them on in the living room."

Dumb Questions

My neighbor asks the dumbest questions. We both live on the top floor of the building and when she gets into the elevator with me she asks, "Going down?"

When I'm sitting by the pool she comes out, pulls over an empty chair and asks, "Is anyone sitting here?"

I wore my new $150 mauve chiffon to the bridge dessert Friday and she told me, "That's a nice style, but do you really like that color?"

I've decided to ignore her. Today she was in the lobby all red-eyed and sniffling. She gulped out, "I just came from Ada Trent's funeral."

"Oh," I said. "Did she die?"

—Rhoda Riddell

The Sweet Truth

O. Henry's name was coined, it's true,
Not just to make it shorter.
Can you imagine candy bars
Called William Sydney Porter?

—Donald R. Williams

"Same old breakfast, same old job, same old drive home—give me the usual."

Vital Assist

Sometimes people are so helpful
I simply can't believe it,
Like when I can't find something
And they ask, "Where did you leave it?"

—Arnold J. Zarett

Tailgating Peril

Sign on the back of a newspaper truck: "Don't follow too closely—you may end up in the newspapers."

—Alphonse Simonaitis

A Thought on Horses

When you lead a horse to water and you can make him drink but he never stops drinking, then is not that your hour of whoa?

—*Olof Dahlskog*

Handyman

No matter how tough the job
He never quits in despair;
He'll stay right with it
Till it's fixed beyond repair.

—*Homer Phillips*

The Waiting Game

When eating out I sometimes find
The service couldn't be later.
The names I think are quite confused—
It's I who am the waiter.

—*Lois Leurgans*

"So what if the cost of living does go up another ten percent? It's still worth it, isn't it?"

Get the Picture?

No one will ever consider me
Particularly profound.
The trouble is, when my mind goes blank,
I forget to turn off the sound.

—May Richstone

A Corker

The customs agent poked through an old gentleman's luggage and found a bottle of wine. "I thought you said there was nothing in here but clothing," he said.

"That's true," said the old gent. "That there's my nightcap!"

—Lucille Harper

Collector's Item

Effective immediately a new tax will be withheld from your paycheck. This is a tax to pay the cost of collecting all other taxes. If the tax amounts to more than the balance of your check, you will be billed for the difference.

—Buzz Cardozo

Evictus

Rain, rain, go away,
You've filled the hole where I stay,
And lying out here on the lawn,
I feel a robin coming on!

—William Wormswords

The Strange Case of The Bulky Billfold

My wallet, once flat, has now become fat,
 Although I've not recently fed it;
It's grossly distended with cards, all intended
 To make me go broke via credit.

—Dick Emmons